SEA CREATURES

SEYMOUR SIMON

HARPER

An Imprint of HarperCollinsPublishers

*In memory of Rachel Carson, scientist, naturalist,
and author, whose book* The Sea Around Us
so influenced me to become a writer.

Special thanks to Robinson W. Fulweiler

Photo Credits

Page 2: © D.P. Wilson / FLPA / Science Source; page 4: © Georgette Douwma /
naturepl.com; page 7: © Alex Mustard / naturepl.com; page 8: © Steve Trewhella
/ FLPA / Science Source; page 9: © Dr. Paul Zahl / Science Source; page 11: ©
Manfred Kage / Science Source; page 12: © Kim Taylor / naturepl.com; page 14:
© David Tipling / naturepl.com; page 15: © Steven Kazlowski / SeaPics.com; page
17: © Steven Kovacs / SeaPics.com; page 18: © Andrea Izzotti / Shutterstock; page
20: © Sergey Uryadnikov / Shutterstock; page 21: © Georgette Douwma / Science
Source; page 23: © Asther Lau Choon Siew / dreamstime.com; page 24: © Aleksey
Stemmer / Shutterstock; page 27, right to left: © Scubazoo / Science Source; ©
Christoph Gerigk / Science Source; page 28: © Whitcomberd / dreamstime.com;
page 31: © Alex Mustard / naturepl.com; page 32: © Pedro Narra / naturepl.com;
page 35, top left to bottom right: © David Shale / naturepl.com; © Dave Forcucci
/ SeaPics.com; © Danté Fenolio / Science Source; © Steve Downer / Science
Source; © Danté Fenolio / Science Source; page 36, counterclockwise: © David
Shale / naturepl.com; © NOAA/Monterey Bay Aquarium Research Institute; © A.
Fifis/Ifremer; pages 38–39, left to right: © Science Source. Colorization by Robin
Treadwell; © Expedition to the Deep Slope/NOAA/OER.

Library of Congress Control Number: 2017949550
ISBN 978-0-06-228921-6 (trade bdg.) — ISBN 978-0-06-228920-9 (pbk.)

18 19 20 21 22 SCP 10 9 8 7 6 5 4 3 2 1
❖
First Edition

Author's Note

From a young age, I was interested in animals, space, my surroundings—all the natural sciences. When I was a teenager, I became the president of a nationwide junior astronomy club with a thousand members. After college, I became a classroom teacher for nearly twenty-five years while also writing articles and books for children on science and nature even before I became a full-time writer. My experience as a teacher gives me the ability to understand how to reach my young readers and get them interested in the world around us.

I've written more than 300 books, and I've thought a lot about different ways to encourage interest in the natural world, as well as how to show the joys of nonfiction. When I write, I use comparisons to help explain unfamiliar ideas, complex concepts, and impossibly large numbers. I try to engage your senses and imagination to set the scene and to make science fun. For example, in *Penguins*, I emphasize the playful nature of these creatures on the very first page by mentioning how penguins excel at swimming and diving. I use strong verbs to enhance understanding. I make use of descriptive detail and ask questions that anticipate what you may be thinking (sometimes right at the start of the book).

Many of my books are photo-essays, which use extraordinary photographs to amplify and expand the text, creating different and engaging ways of exploring nonfiction. You'll also find a glossary, an index, and website and research recommendations in most of my books, which make them ideal for enhancing your reading and learning experience. As William Blake wrote in his poem, I want my readers "to see a world in a grain of sand, / And a heaven in a wild flower, / Hold infinity in the palm of your hand, / And eternity in an hour."

Seymour Simon

A colorful nudibranch, a soft-bodied sea slug

Sea creatures come in all shapes and sizes. There are some sea creatures with no eyes and others with dozens of them. Some have many arms and others have none at all. There are those that look like brightly colored flowers and others that look like dragons. Some are as small as the period at the end of this sentence. Others are about as big as your hand or foot. But a blue whale may be bigger than a school bus and weigh as much as twenty African elephants. In any case, all living things in nature have much the same needs. They must have food, adjust to their surroundings, and be able to survive.

The **sea**, in which so many creatures exist, is not the same all over the world; nor is it the same at the surface as it is at the bottom of the sea. Seawater varies in temperature and saltiness from place to place. Sunlight lights up the surface waters, but no sunlight can penetrate the dark depths of the sea. Waves and currents constantly churn surface waters, but water currents in the depths take centuries to move from polar regions to the equator. Yet wherever we look in the seas—from dark, icy polar waters to bright, warm tropical seas, from seashore to open waters to ocean floor—we find life.

One part of the sea can be very different from another part. The upper 656 feet is called the sunlight zone. In this zone, green plants or other green organisms live near the surface of the waters where sunlight enters. Green living things need sunlight to live and grow, which then become food for other animals. Because of this, the sunlight zone is home to most of the fishes, mammals, and turtles that live in the sea.

Rarely, sunlight enters the depths of the sea beyond 656 feet. The zone between 656 feet and 3,280 feet is called the twilight zone. Even deeper, the midnight zone is below 3,280 feet. Animals living at these depths must feed on food that drifts down from surface waters. Many deep-sea creatures, such as the giant isopod and the vampire squid, look strange and mysterious, almost as if they come from alien planets.

Sea creatures live in the cold waters of polar regions as well as in the warm waters of the tropics. Some live in waters that change temperatures during winter and summer. Still others live along shores where they are covered by the tides for only a few hours each day. Each kind of animal is best fitted to survive in particular surroundings. A cold-water creature cannot survive in the tropics, and a shore animal cannot survive in the open ocean.

A bigfin squid hovering in the sea at night

Sea anemone with tentacles extended

Life in the sea reproduces in many different ways. Some sea organisms split, forming two living things out of one. Often these animals and plants are small, many too tiny to be seen without a magnifying lens or a microscope. But some are much bigger than you imagine.

In the Mariana Trench, seven miles below the surface of the Pacific Ocean, scientists found large **amoebas**. These single-celled creatures, called **xenophyophores**, are only found in deep seas. They often grow up to four inches long.

Sea **anemones** and **corals** can reproduce by budding. Small parts of their bodies grow outward, break off from the parent, and form a new animal. Some fish such as the female gray grouper scatter millions of eggs in the water over a year, and only a few might survive to become adults.

Other sea animals lay fewer eggs and care for them. The female sea horse safeguards her eggs by placing them in a pouch in front of the male. The eggs develop in the pouch until they hatch into baby sea horses.

In the sea, as on land, animals depend on plants and other green organisms for food. Only green plants and green organisms can make the sugar and other food nutrients that all living creatures need to survive. All animals eat plants directly or eat other animals that feed on green life.

You may have seen large green seaweeds that grow in the sea along many shores. These large seaweeds make up less than 1 percent of the plants that live in the oceans. The vast majority of sea plants float in the sunlit surface waters and are too small to be seen without a magnifying lens. They are called **phytoplankton**, from the Greek words *phyto*, meaning "plant," and *plankton*, meaning "drifting." Phytoplankton make up the pastures of the sea.

Most of these tiny green organisms are one-celled **diatoms**. A diatom is enclosed in a shell like a box with a lid. The coverings are rock-hard and protect the diatoms. Many diatoms are oddly shaped and have spines that help them float. Different kinds of diatoms live in different parts of the seas. But a diatom living in warm regions would die in cold regions.

The sea has seasons just as does the land. The underwater spring season has more hours of sun, and diatoms and other green organisms double in numbers each day. At times, the sea may be dyed green, yellow, or brown with their colors.

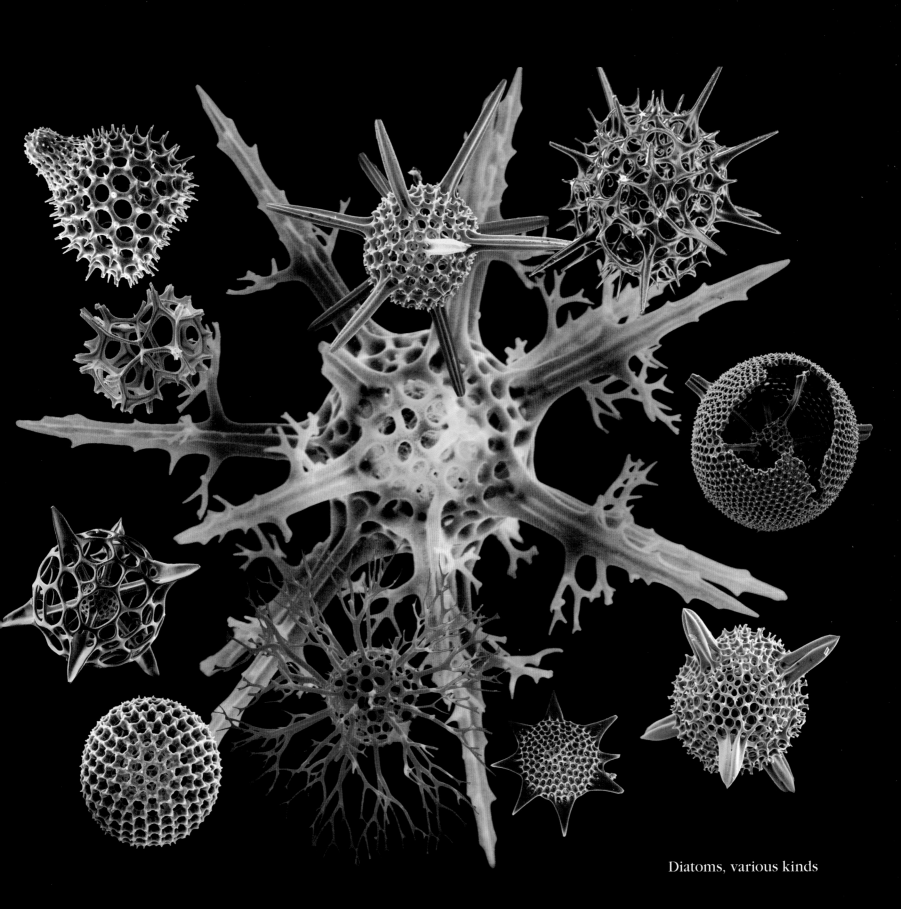

Diatoms, various kinds

Copepods gathering to feed

Billions upon billions of diatoms provide rich feeding for tiny animals, **zooplankton**, that live in the sea. Zooplankton are usually a bit larger than phytoplankton and come in many kinds and shapes. Some are tiny, while others are larger and include newly hatched young of fish, shrimp, and many other sea animals.

Plankton animals and plants are eaten by slightly larger organisms called **copepods**, about the size of pinheads. These look like tiny shrimp with feathery feet. Copepods in turn are eaten by small fish such as sardines and herrings, and these are eaten by larger fish such as tunas and sharks.

You can think of the life in the sea as a food chain or a food web: phytoplankton, zooplankton, herring, tuna. For a tuna to gain one pound, it must eat ten pounds of smaller fish such as herrings. Ten pounds of herring live on a hundred pounds of copepods, which in turn need a thousand pounds of plankton food. At the end, for a tuna, atop the food chain, to gain one pound, one thousand pounds of plankton are needed at the bottom of the food chain. Sea creatures are part of many different food chains in a web of life. Each chain begins with phytoplankton that produce food and ends with a few larger animals that feed on smaller animals and plants.

Krill

The cold waters of the Arctic and Antarctic Oceans (**oceans** are larger than seas) are mineral rich and have large populations of sea life, more than any other of the world's oceans. Food chains in the Antarctic often involve seabirds and sea mammals that rest and breed on the edges of the surrounding lands.

The Antarctic seas contain a rich pasture of diatoms. Huge numbers of krill, small, shrimplike animals, feed on the diatoms. In turn, the krill are eaten by small fish and different kinds of penguins such as the emperor and Adélie. Penguins' bodies make them excellent swimmers because they are streamlined for underwater movement. When swimming underwater, the penguins need to surface only every now and then for a quick breath of air.

Leopard seals are fierce hunters and the second largest seal in the Antarctic. They feed on penguins and the young of other seals. In turn, leopard seals are preyed on by orcas, or killer whales. The thirty-foot-long killer whale has forty-eight strong, sharp teeth set in a powerful jaw.

Baleen whales are in a much shorter food chain. They feed directly on krill, straining them from the waters through thin, horny plates of keratin (like your nails) called baleen. Krill feed directly on plankton. It takes one hundred pounds of plankton to make a pound of a baleen whale. But a pound of killer whale needs ten thousand pounds of plankton in its food chain.

Leopard seal and penguins on an iceberg

Sea creatures depend on their senses to find food, avoid enemies, have young, and carry on other life activities. They see, hear, smell, touch, and taste, but very differently from the ways people use their senses.

Sight is an important sense that animals use to survive. A common sea scallop has up to forty tiny blue eyes ringing its shell. It can see an enemy coming from any direction. The scallop snaps its shell open and closed, which results in a series of leaps and bounds that move it out of danger. The Atlantic bay scallop has thirty to forty blue eyes along the margin of its shell that help it see movement and shadows and detect **predators**. Even the jellyfish has a number of eyespots around its umbrella-shaped body. It pulses in the water, moving toward light. Sea worms also have eyespots that respond to light.

Fish, whales, dolphins, squid, and octopuses have eyes that are much like people's eyes. The eyes have adjustable lenses that focus an image on a light-sensitive retina. Each eye is filled with a fluid that helps it keep its round shape. Each animal has a nervous system that sends messages from the eyes to the brain.

When an octopus spots a food animal, such as a crab, it glides smoothly and approaches its prey. About a foot away, it stops and pounces. All sharp-sighted sea animals use their eyes to find food and to flee from danger.

Atlantic bay scallop

Dolphins

Sound travels more than four times faster in water than it does in air, and many kinds of fish have a good sense of hearing. But one sea mammal, the dolphin, uses hearing in a very different way than fish.

Dolphins have long been observed to be able to avoid fishing nets even at night. In experiments, dolphins were shown to respond to sonar (sound waves that are used to tell an object's distance and position). Sonar uses sound waves at pitches too high for humans to hear many of the sounds. Dolphins use sound waves they emit to detect and locate fish, nets, rocks, and other objects around them. They can tell the difference between plastic fish and real fish even in complete darkness. They are able to catch fish in tanks with many obstacles.

Dolphins give off a series of clicks every twenty seconds or so. The sounds bounce off fish and other objects and return to the dolphin. As the dolphin moves in the fish's direction, it turns its head left to right, giving off a volley of clicks. The sounds enable a dolphin to tell the difference between a school of fish and a clump of seaweed and even between two different kinds of fish.

Great white shark in an attack

Another important sense is smell. For example, sharks are able to zero in on a meal from great distances because of their senses of touch and smell. Along a shark's body is a lateral line, a row of nerve endings that are sensitive to any movement of water. Sharks are also extrasensitive to the smell of blood and sense even a tiny amount from a great distance. Salmon use their sense of smell to find their way from the ocean to the very stream in which they were born.

Some sea creatures have no, or almost no, sense of sight. Others have no sense of hearing. But most sea creatures have a sense of touch. Many fish have a lateral line in their head and along both sides of their bodies that detects movement and vibration in the surrounding waters. Fish use their lateral lines to sense prey and predators.

Even simple sea animals such as **sponges** and anemones draw away if you touch them. The sea squirt, for example, is a sac-shaped animal filled with jelly and has two short, open tubes. One tube pulls in water and the other tube squirts it out. The sea squirt has no eyes, nose, or ears. Yet if you touch it, it squirts out a jet of water that makes it move away.

Sea animals have other senses. Many can tell up from down so that they can return to an upright position after being tossed around by surf or waves. Some can tell slight differences in water temperature. Each of these senses helps the animal to survive.

Sea squirts

One of the best ways to survive in the sea is to avoid being seen. Some sea creatures blend into their surroundings so well that they can't be seen unless they move. Others conceal themselves in rocks or coral formations. Still others such as the octopus and the squid send out a kind of smoke screen and use it as a distraction to escape. The octopus and the squid also can blend in with their surroundings by changing the color of their skins in seconds.

Some deep-sea creatures release a kind of luminous cloud when they are in danger. In the darkness of the sea depths, the bright cloud momentarily blinds the pursuer, and the animal can make its escape.

Most fish and other sea creatures that live in the upper layers of the sea, such as sharks and dolphins, have light-colored undersides and darker backs. When the sea creature is looked at from below, the light coloring blends in with the surface of the water and the sky. But when it is looked at from above, the dark back blends in with the dark sea bottom. This is called **countershading**.

The sargassum fish and the frogfish have colors and bits of skin sticking out that blend in with the sargassum weeds around them. Sargassum fish look exactly like the weeds they live among. Some kinds of frogfish have a bit of skin hanging in front of their mouths that acts like a lure to catch small fish that are their prey.

Frogfish

Clown fish and anemone

The clown fish is a brightly striped little fish that lives in tropical waters. To prevent it from being eaten by predators, the clown fish spends much of the time calmly swimming among the poisonous tentacles of a sea anemone. The clown fish avoids getting stung because it gives off a fluid that prevents the anemone from discharging its stingers. The anemone benefits by having the clown fish around because it attracts larger fish that come close enough and within reach of its tentacles. This kind of partnership where both benefit is called **symbiosis**.

Some fish benefit from their partners without giving much in return. Pilot fish swim close enough to a shark where it is too difficult for the shark to try to take a bite of it. Pilot fish were once thought to guide the shark to food and then feed on the remains of the shark's meal. But the truth is that they only feed on the remains and have nothing to do with guiding the shark. Remoras follow large fish even more closely. A remora "hitchhikes" on a shark by attaching itself with a sucking disk to the top of the shark's head.

Some sea creatures use another animal for protection and food.

The banded coral shrimp, or "barber-pole shrimp," lives in the coral reefs of the Caribbean Sea. It walks around the reefs in plain sight of the nearby swimming fish that might easily feed on it. But the groupers and parrot fishes do not attack the little shrimp. Instead, they swim slowly by and close enough to the shrimp. Then the shrimp steps lightly over the body of the large fish, picking away at the tiny animals that live on its skin. The cleaning helps both the shrimp find food and the fish get rid of parasites.

The largest clams in the world grow to as much as four feet across. These *Tridacna* clams live in the sunny, shallow parts of the coral reefs of the South Pacific Ocean. Each clam has what looks like small, round eyes all around its fleshy mantle. But they really are not eyes at all. They are like small windows into chambers inside the clam. Tiny green algae live inside the chambers. Both the huge clam and the tiny algae benefit from their partnership. The clam gets food nutrients from the algae, and the algae are protected inside the clam. Strange partnerships exist throughout the sea. They all have one common goal: they help sea creatures to survive.

Barber pole shrimp

Tridacna (giant) clam

One kind of pipefish

All the sea creatures and plants along a shore are fitted to their surroundings. Living things of one kind or another are found along almost every shoreline in the world. Sandy shores or rocky shores, big tides or small tides, rough surf or calm seas, all support some kind of life.

Shore creatures on rocky shores must be able to withstand the force of waves crashing on the rocks. Many do this by cementing themselves onto the rocks, like barnacles, or holding on with a muscular foot, like snails, or with many tiny tube feet ending in suckers, like starfish.

Along the shore on sandy beaches you can find all kinds of crabs, sea urchins, and whelks. Although the breaking waves bring the crabs food, the waves also threaten to wash the crabs out to sea. Their armored bodies protect them against the force of the surf.

Plants, such as eelgrass, take root on muddy shores. The waving strands of grass offer shelter for sea horses, pipefish, shrimp, and young fish. Worms and clams live in the rich mud. The forces of waves and sunlight all combine to make different living conditions for countless kinds of sea creatures to survive.

Salmon, cod, mackerel, eels, seals, whales, green turtles, and hosts of other sea creatures travel on regular seasonal paths known as migrations. The long journey is part of the animal's life cycle. There are many differences among migratory sea creatures. Some make their journey many times while others go but once. Some travel thousands of miles; others travel much shorter distances. There are two main ways that migrations help the animals. One way is that when animals migrate they may find a place to mate and reproduce. The other reason is that there are seasonal changes in the food supply, and the animals travel to where more food is available.

The great migration of the Pacific salmon begins in the spring. After hatching in small freshwater streams, millions of fingerlings travel down the rivers of the Northwest into the sea. In the sea, they travel far from shore. Some kinds of salmon make a two-thousand-mile journey, while others may travel ten thousand miles before returning. Incredibly, salmon are able to find the same river and stream from which they came years before. Both male and female salmon live for only a few days after spawning.

Pacific salmon spawning

Green sea turtle on beach at night

In early spring in the South Atlantic Ocean, female green sea turtles swim steadily toward Ascension Island, a five-mile-wide speck of land fourteen hundred miles off the coast of Brazil. Once arriving on the beach, the female turtle moves up the shore and lays seventy-five to two hundred eggs in a hole she has hollowed out of the sand with her flippers. After covering the eggs with sand, she leaves the eggs alone and goes back to the sea.

The eggs are warmed by the sun and hatch after about two months. Then the hatchlings will go back to the sea. But there are many dangers they will have to face. Young turtles are preyed on by birds, small mammals, and other predators. Some hatchlings lose their way back to the waters. For the young that reach the ocean waters, it will be ten to twenty-five years before they are old enough to breed.

By June, the beaches are deserted. The three-hundred-fifty-pound adult turtles have departed, and the young are gone. Scientists have tagged the adult turtles to find out where they go after nesting. Many feed at sea off the coast of Brazil.

But after two or three years, some of the tagged adult turtles begin to return. Not only do they come back to the island, but they return to the very beach on which they had originally laid their eggs. No one knows for sure how the turtles find their way through hundreds of miles of ocean waters back to such a specific location.

ost of the sea creatures we know live along the shores where water meets land and in the upper sunlit zone of the open ocean. But more than 60 percent of our planet is covered by seawater more than a mile deep, and it is largely unexplored. Here are some of the strange creatures we have found there:

- **Anglerfish:** Anglerfish have huge heads and giant mouths filled with sharp teeth. The females have a piece of their bodies hanging above their mouths like a fishing pole. Tipped with a lure of luminous flesh, it brings in prey close enough to be caught.

- **Lantern fish:** A deep-water fish that gets its name because it can produce light in the dark ocean depths. The light is given off by tiny organs in the fish in a chemical process known as bioluminescence.

- **Fangtooth fish:** The scary-looking fangtooth is only about six inches long, but its teeth are the largest compared to its body size of any animal in the world.

- **Vampire squid:** Living two miles below the surface, these small sea creatures have eyes that are the largest of any animal on Earth compared to its size. They can draw their dark, webbed arms over themselves like a vampire's cloak.

- **Giant isopod:** Looking like an alien in a science fiction story, this deep-sea creature is related to the small pill bugs you can spot in the grass in the summer.

Lantern fish

Fangtooth fish

Anglerfish

Vampire squid

Giant isopod

Deep-sea cirrate octopus

Yeti crab

Giant jellyfish,
nicknamed "Big Red"

The Census of Marine Life is an ongoing international project that seeks to identify and record all the sea creatures in all the oceans of the world. Thousands of scientists from more than eighty nations are contributing to the Census. Here are only a few of their findings:

On a deep-sea research mission, scientists found a remarkable "hairy" crab on the ocean floor. They nicknamed it the "yeti crab" after the Abominable Snowman, or yeti, a hairy, apelike legendary creature said to live in the Himalaya Mountains. The yeti crab is also part of a newly discovered family of crustaceans (animals related to crabs, lobsters, and shrimp).

This giant jellyfish, nicknamed "Big Red," was found at depths of two thousand to four thousand feet across the Pacific Ocean in seabeds near California, Hawaii, and Japan. Big Red can grow to thirty inches in diameter.

This kind of octopus is bioluminescent; it glows in the dark. Light-emitting spots in its mouth are thought to attract prey animals and lead them inward. The octopus is fairly common across the North Atlantic Ocean. Can you think of a good nickname for a lighted octopus?

From early times people explored the oceans and created stories and myths about sea creatures. They told stories of the kraken—a sea creature like a giant squid or octopus with many arms. Some said the kraken was the size of an island and could pull a large sailing ship under the water with its arms. We've never discovered such a creature, and even a giant squid or giant octopus is considerably smaller than the mythical kraken.

Most people don't believe these old stories about giant animals and other strange sea creatures. Still, fewer explorers have descended to the deepest parts of the oceans than space explorers have walked on the moon. And even now, we are still discovering amazing new sea creatures and startling facts about the water world under the waves.

Drawing of a legendary giant octopus

Photo of octopus on a deep-ocean submersible

GLOSSARY

Amoebas—Small one-celled living things with jellylike bodies that change shape.

Anemones—Small, predatory sea creatures with many tentacles that are named after the land flower, the anemone.

Copepods—A group of tiny, hard-shelled animals found mostly in the oceans.

Coral—Small sea creatures whose skeletons form coral rock.

Countershading—Protective coloration of some animals in which parts seen from below are light (like the sky) and parts seen from above are dark (like the sea bottom).

Diatoms—Small single-celled water plants that have a shell composed of a hard mineral called silica.

Ocean—A large, connected body of saltwater that covers almost three-fourths of Earth's surface.

Phyto—Relating to plants.

Phytoplankton—Microscopic green plants that live in the light-filled reaches of the sea and provide food for many sea animals.

Plankton—Tiny animals and plants that live in the oceans.

Predators—Animals that prey on other animals.

Sea—A large body of saltwater somewhat smaller than an ocean. Usually surrounded almost entirely by land.

Sponges—Primitive, many-celled sea creatures that have no muscles, hearts, or brains.

Symbiosis—Interaction between two different living things physically close to each other, usually to the advantage of both.

Xenophyophores—Large, deep-sea, single-celled animals (like amoebas).

Zooplankton—Small animals that float in ocean waters.

INDEX

Bold type indicates illustrations.

READ MORE ABOUT IT

Seymour Simon's website
www.seymoursimon.com

The Census of Marine Life
www.coml.org/about-census
www.oceanexplorer.noaa.gov/
projects/02census

**Office of Protected Resources –
NOAA Fisheries**
www.nmfs.noaa.gov/pr/
education/kids.htm